An Englishman in N.Y.

Bites on the Big Apple

Colin Joyce

NHK Publishing

An Englishman in N.Y.
Bites on the Big Apple

Copyright © 2011 by Colin Joyce
ISBN 978-4-14-035097-3 C0082

All rights reserved. Published in Japan by NHK Publishing, Inc. (NHK Shuppan)

No part of this book may be used or reproduced in any manner whatsoever without written permission, except in the case of brief quotations embodied in critical articles and reviews.

For information:
NHK Publishing, Inc. (NHK Shuppan)
41-1 Udagawa-cho, Shibuya, Tokyo, 150-8081, Japan
http://www.nhk-book.co.jp

Printed in Japan

Book Design by Takeshi Hatanaka
Proofreading by Mariko Kakehi

An Englishman in N.Y.

Bites on the Big Apple

CONTENTS

Preface — 7

Subway Culture — 10

Brooklyn Is Best — 15

Tipping Dilemmas — 21

Naming New York — 27

A Tea Drinker in a Coffee City — 33

An Oasis in the City — 38

Why "the Big Apple" Isn't "the Big Chestnut" — 43

Polish New York — 48

Emergency? Call 911 Fed Up? Call 311 — 54

Why Is Everyone Being So Nice to Me?	59
The Oxford-New York Dictionary, Part One	65
The Oxford-New York Dictionary, Part Two	71
Historical Titbits About New York	76
How I Became "Litigious"	82
Treasure Hunting in Brooklyn	88
The Uninsured Life	93
Some of My Least Favourite Americanisms	98
Some of My Favourite Americanisms	104

CONTENTS

The Great Sunday Times Reading Challenge — 109

Damn You, Seinfeld — 114

World Cup Woes — 119

My Personal Ten Best Things About Living in New York — 124

My Personal Ten Worst Things About Living in New York — 130

The Joys of Storage — 137

Mind the Gap — 142

PREFACE

I once met a man who told me he was a New Yorker from Ohio. He explained to me that "everyone" in New York was ultimately from somewhere else, whether that be four generations ago or a few years ago (as in his case). So, in his view, if you lived there you were entitled to claim to be a New Yorker.

It didn't work that way for me. Partly it was because I never intended to stay in New York. But I also think it was largely because I was English; I already had an identity that stubbornly refused to melt away, even if I had wanted it to.

That isn't to say I didn't find New York fascinating. It could be alien and infuriating at times, but it was often wonderful and always interesting. To rephrase Samuel Johnson, a man who isn't interested in New York isn't interested in life.

This collection of essays is not an attempt to give a comprehensive view of life in New York. Nor do I claim that I represent the English as whole when I am writing. I wrote the pieces over the course of three quite unusual years and they reflect my personal experience of trying to learn about and adapt to life in a city I had always been curious about. I pursued topics and wrote almost "as I please". I only hope that it is of interest to readers too.

Attentive readers may notice some apparent inconsistencies. For example, that I claim to live in three or four different places. This reflects the fact that the essays were produced at the pace of one per month over three years—during which I moved frequently—and we have decided to publish them without changes, as my "live take" on New York.

Takeshi Nakano and Namiko Okumura of NHK Publishing were a great help and encouragement to me during the work on these essays and this book. Any errors of fact or interpretation are of course my own.

I was informed that people who followed these essays when they were first published in NHK *Radio Eikawa* texts found them difficult to read. I can only apologise that I never learned to express myself well in simple English, and thank everyone who made the effort to read them anyway. It's a great compliment to think that anyone would care to read my thoughts, let alone when there is a big language barrier.

I left New York in 2010 and moved back to England. I never became a "New Yorker from England", but I think about the place all the time. Reading these essays again reminded me of how much I miss it, so I guess New York became part of me.

Subway Culture

The New York subway system is in many ways a mirror of the city itself. It is impressive and fascinating but can also be wildly illogical and sometimes just plain strange.

People sometimes say that "New York is not really America", meaning that it is very different from the rest of the country. Certainly that is true in terms of public transport. In a country where the car is king, New York relies heavily on an extensive subway system.

The network stretches all the way from the Bronx, in northern New York, to Coney Island, in southern Brooklyn. The longest train line runs for over 30 miles.

There are exactly 26 lines, by coincidence the same number as letters in the alphabet. But, for some reason, when they named the lines they skipped out certain letters such as H and P, used the letter S three times, and numbered the rest 1 to 7.

The annual total of riders exceeds London or Paris, but is still only half that of Tokyo. But the New York subway has certain qualities that other subways lack. For one thing, New Yorkers can take the subway to the beach (either Coney Island or Rockaway Beach). Also, the fare for a single ride is $2 regardless of the distance, so it is a relative bargain for long-distance commuters. The system runs 24 hours, a real boon to late-night revellers. And the platforms are generally not as deep underground as London or Tokyo, making it quicker and easier to step on and off.

But sometimes the subway here can seem amazingly primitive. Delays and station closures

Vocabulary

the Bronx ブロンクス［NY市北部の自治区］
Coney Island コニーアイランド［NY市東部ブルックリン地区にある保養地］
relative bargain 相対的に得であること
boon 恩恵
reveller 酒盛りする人

are regular problems. Last summer heavy rain caused much of the system to shut down during morning rush hour. And commuters stranded on platforms were unable to call their offices as stations do not have mobile phone coverage.

Station names are erratic. One large station in Brooklyn for example is called Atlantic Avenue if you are on the Q train but is called Pacific Street if you are on the R train. In Manhattan meanwhile there are four separate stations with the same name—Canal Street—situated along the length of that road. Perhaps for this reason when asking for directions in New York you don't ask "Which is the way to 14th Street station?" but rather "Which way to the 6 train?"

It can still be confusing once you make it to the platform. There are no electronic signs giving estimates of when the next train will arrive. After a few minutes people will automatically begin to lean over and peer down the tunnels, impatiently looking for their train. Occasionally something utterly bizarre will happen, such as a 3 train arriving on a 4 train platform, or an uptown train arriving on a downtown platform. Little bits of paper plastered on the walls of the subway sometimes warn you of such irregularities but few people ever read them.

Much like New Yorkers in general, the people you meet in the subway can be amazing or annoying. There are three main types of nuisances: beggars, hawkers selling candy or pirated DVDs and religious freaks shouting about Jesus.

On the other hand, the stations often have very high quality performers. One of the drawbacks of subway rides is the lack of contact

Vocabulary
strand 立ち往生する
erratic 気まぐれな
utterly bizarre まったく奇怪な
hawker 行商人
drawback 欠点、不利益

with the life of the city as you go through it. But in New York you might find a busker playing cool jazz at a station in Greenwich Village. At Canal Street in Chinatown someone will be playing an erhu (a traditional two-stringed Chinese instrument). In Franklin Avenue—a black neighbourhood in Brooklyn—it will be Caribbean steel drums.

Famously, the Mayor of New York Michael Bloomberg uses the subway to commute to City Hall. Less famously, he doesn't do so every day and is often chauffeured several miles to a station where he can get an express that requires no change of trains. But the message is clear anyway: if you're a real New Yorker you ride the subway.

Vocabulary
busker　大道芸人
erhu　二胡
black neighbourhood　黒人居住地区
be chauffeured　お抱え運転手に運転してもらう

Brooklyn Is Best

Americans sometimes tell you that if Brooklyn were a city—instead of one of the five boroughs of New York—it would be the country's fourth biggest city. As a fan of Brooklyn I would go further than that: it might be America's best city. Certainly I think it does many things better than Manhattan.

Yes, Manhattan has a lot of attractions. But they can all be reached from Brooklyn. Meanwhile Brooklyn has nicer apartments at lower prices, quieter neighbourhoods and more sunlight (many people in Manhattan live their lives in the shadow of those high-rise buildings).

Vocabulary
borough NY市の自治区

Brooklyn has never been developed as ruthlessly as Manhattan. It's said that New York is a good city for walking—but only in Brooklyn is it really nice to stroll. Brooklyn neighbourhoods such as Park Slope, Carroll Gardens and Brooklyn Heights are far more beautiful and pleasant than their Manhattan counterparts.

In places Brooklyn resembles Victorian London: whole rows of stately four-storey houses, except the material is the famous American "brownstone" rather than London redbrick. (Just as in London, buildings that once housed a single family are now split into separate floors. And even the basements and lofts are converted to squeeze in extra apartments.)

Brooklyn was, in fact, once an independent city. It voted to become part of New York only in 1894, just over a decade after the completion of the fantastic Brooklyn Bridge. Sure, it made sense. But it also cemented Brooklyn's status as the "little brother" of Manhattan. I wish more people would see Brooklyn for what it is: a vibrant, lively and fascinating place.

For the record, if Brooklyn were independent it would be fourth behind New York, Los Angeles and Chicago. But it would be bigger than San Francisco, Seattle, Boston and Washington DC combined. Brooklyn would also likely be America's most ethnically diverse city: it has particularly large populations of Orthodox Jews, West Indians and Russians. Manhattan by contrast is increasingly white and middle class.

Many famous people have made their homes in Brooklyn, including writers such as

Vocabulary
ruthlessly 無慈悲に、容赦なく
Brooklyn Heights ブルックリンハイツ［ブルックリンの閑静な高級住宅地］
stately four-storey house 壮麗な4階建ての家
convert 改装する
Orthodox Jew 正統派ユダヤ教徒

Norman Mailer, Truman Capote and Arthur Miller. The composers Aaron Copland and George Gershwin lived here as did the film directors Woody Allen and Spike Lee. Curiously, though, Brooklyn has not been very lovingly portrayed in film. (Woody Allen's tribute to life in New York is called *Manhattan*, for example.)

Importantly for an Englishman, Brooklyn is a better place to drink than Manhattan. It has a superb brewery, the Brooklyn Brewery, which produces an excellent range of beers: hefeweizen, IPA, winter ale, brown ale. Every Friday the brewery opens its doors and sells beers fresh from the production line. Brooklyn also has better bars. My personal favourite is the Brooklyn Inn, with high ceilings and a long oak bar something like a classic English pub.

Brooklyn has many highlights. Prospect Park was designed by the same partnership (Frederick Law Olmsted and Calbert Vaux) who earlier created Central Park. I like to think they had gained experience as Prospect Park is more lovely (and less crowded).

Not far away is the delightful Botanic Garden, within which lies a particularly attractive Japanese garden dating back to 1915. Unlike Japanese gardens in England from the same period, this one was the work of a Japanese immigrant: Takeo Shiota, a native of Chiba who had an office on Fifth Avenue in Manhattan.

And then there is Coney Island, the historic beach and amusement park. Every year on Independence Day it hosts one of America's most iconic events: the speed-eating hot dog contest.

Vocabulary
superb brewery すばらしい醸造所
hefeweizen ヘーフェヴァイツェン [白ビール]
IPA インディア・ペール・エール
long oak bar カシの木の長いカウンター

An Englishman in N.Y.

Green-Wood Cemetery in Brooklyn is among the most peaceful and greenest I have ever visited. Here one can find the final resting place of such diverse figures as Jean-Michel Basquiat, the Brooklyn-born artist, and "Bill the Butcher", a notorious streetfighter who inspired the Martin Scorcese film *Gangs of New York*. Nearby lies the grave of Townshend Harris, the first consul of the US to Japan.

There is one other great thing about Brooklyn: the Manhattan skyline. When you are actually in Manhattan you can't really see it. If you want to enjoy the view of Manhattan, you really ought to pop across the river to Brooklyn Heights.

Tipping Dilemmas

Of all the unusual customs in the US, none is such a regular—if low level—annoyance as tipping. On an average day you usually have to decide whether to tip and how much at least once. Probably more often.

You can't reasonably just decide never to tip. A lot of waitresses are paid below the minimum wage so, by not tipping, you are denying them the chance of a decent standard of living.

Different scenarios require different levels of tipping. In a restaurant you tip between 15 percent and 20 percent. In a bar you generally tip a dollar for each drink. So far, so simple.

Vocabulary
decent （収入などが）人並みの

But it can get confusing: How much do you tip at a self-service buffet? You were brought water and your table was wiped down but not much else. At a bar do you revert to 15 percent if your drinks are brought to your table?

Tipping is a pain for people weak at mental arithmetic. The last few blocks in a taxi are stressful for me as I try to estimate how much I will need to tip even as the fare on the meter keeps changing.

One short cut to calculate a middling tip is to double the amount of sales tax, which is always written on the check. This works well in New York where the tax is 8.875 percent. But you have to remember the sales tax is only 7 percent just across the water in New Jersey.

In theory, tipping should reflect the quality of service thereby creating an incentive for good work. But as often as not, people tip generously so as not to look mean in front of others. Or even to show off that the extra few dollars makes no difference to them. People might also tip well at busy places, especially ones they visit regularly. In effect they are "bidding" to receive preferential treatment over other customers, which is different from rewarding good service.

There is an interesting dynamic towards "tip inflation". Fifteen percent used to be the norm and 20 percent was a reward for excellent service. But increasingly 20 percent is the norm. You also see tip jars springing up in places they never used to be, such as counters in coffee shops.

Vocabulary
revert to... …に逆戻りする
mental arithmetic 暗算
middling 並みの
look mean けちに見える
bid （競売などで）値をつける、競る
preferential treatment 差別的な待遇

In expensive establishments you are likely to find various demands made on your wallet. It is wise to have a supply of dollar bills. You have to tip to leave your coat in the cloakroom and might find the doorman expects a tip for running out and hailing a taxi for you.

Sometimes you are expected to tip for services you don't want. Hotel staff might make you leave your suitcase at the front desk even though you could easily wheel it the few extra feet to the elevator. This can be irritating when it takes 10 minutes for your bags to follow you up. A friend from England remembers how the bellhop refused to leave the room until tipped. The problem was she had no American money yet and her friend had jumped into the shower.

Tipping is generally prevalent in places where people feel comfortable with large divergences of wealth and status. Hence it is almost non-existent in Japan but an everyday interaction in New York.

Handing over cash, at the discretion of the giver, strikes me as a cold demonstration of economic reality here: some people have lots of money while others have to run around trying to please them to get some of it from them.

Personally, what bothers me about tipping is the unfairness of it. A waitress in a cheap diner might provide exceptional service but is still only looking at a $4 tip on a $20 lunch. An indifferent waitress can expect $15 or more at an expensive place.

Vocabulary

establishment　施設 [学校、病院、会社、店舗など]
prevalent　一般に行われている
divergence　分岐、相違
at the discretion of...　…の考えしだいで
indifferent　冷淡な

Why should coffee shop employees, who are often middle-class students, get tips while fast-food workers from poorer backgrounds get none? It is common knowledge that good-looking waitresses get more tips. Even more alarming, there is evidence to suggest that white people get tipped significantly more than black people for the same work.

There seems little prospect that the culture of tipping can be ended or even reformed. In the meantime all you can do is try to tip fairly. And get your sums right.

Vocabulary
alarming 驚くべき

Naming New York

I have always been fascinated by place names and what these reveal about the history and character of a place. In this respect New York is not a disappointment.

New York, of course, wasn't always New York. When it was ruled by the Dutch it was called New Amsterdam. It received its present name in 1664 when the English took over.

The Dutch have left their mark elsewhere though. The Bronx, one of the boroughs of New York is believed to derive from the name of a Dutchman, Jonas Bronk, who had a farm in the area 350 years ago.

Brooklyn comes from Breuckelen, which was a town in the Netherlands. The Dutch were the first Europeans to settle in that area. When the English moved in they attempted to rename it Kings County, though this name is not widely used today.

Other names remind us that the original inhabitants were Native Americans. Manhattan comes from Mannahatta ("island of many hills" in the local dialect), while Gowanus (an area in Brooklyn) is named after a local tribal leader.

Many of New York's districts have dull, descriptive names: Midtown, Upper West Side etc. But others are highly inventive. Hell's Kitchen is the name of an area that was once particularly tough (the hottest place in any house is the kitchen, so hell's kitchen must be the worst of the worst).

Dumbo apparently stands for Down Under the Manhattan Bridge Overpass. Tribeca is the Triangle Below Canal (Street) and Nolita is North of Little Italy. It's a bit like the way words are cut and combined in Japanese (*deji-kame* etc.).

Similarly there is Soho, which stands for South of Houston (Street). Coincidentally, there is also a Soho in London but the origin of the name is completely different. The area was once open land where the old fox hunting cry "Soho!" might be heard. Hence the name.

Manhattan is famous for its grid system with numbered avenues running north to south and numbered streets running east to west. This makes the city easier to navigate but less interesting to the name spotter.

Happily for me, the numbering system doesn't apply south of Houston Street. In the southernmost tip of Manhattan, the oldest part of the city, many streets bear very English-sounding names: John Street, Maiden Lane, Broad Street...

Vocabulary
inhabitant 居住者
tribal leader （部族の）首長
inventive 創意に富んだ
grid （街路の）碁盤目
name spotter 名前を言い当てる（のが好きな）人

Perhaps the most famous is Wall Street, home of the New York Stock Exchange and synonymous worldwide with high finance. But it is also a very historic street; it was here in 1789 that George Washington was inaugurated as the first president of the United States (on my birthday as it happens).

Wall Street was so named because the city's defensive wall once stood here. Looking at a map of New York today, with the city stretching over ten miles to the north, it is hard to believe the New Amsterdam settlement was once squeezed into the tiny area below Wall Street.

The name Times Square amuses me because it isn't a proper square at all, just an open area where two avenues cross. (Nor is it any longer home to the New York Times building from which it took its name.)

Some streets have a second name attached to them, usually something descriptive. One part of Seventh Avenue is also called Fashion

Avenue to reflect its history as a garment district. My favourite is Canyon of Heroes, the bottom part of Broadway, so called because it is here that ticker-tape parades honouring sporting and other heroes are held.

Avenue of the Immigrants on the Lower East Side is named in tribute to generations of poverty-stricken immigrants whose first homes were often in the area's crowded tenements.

Before being admitted to New York millions of newcomers passed through the immigration depot on Ellis Island (named after the Welshman Samuel Ellis who once owned it). Next to Ellis Island stands the Statue of Liberty on the

Vocabulary
be inaugurated as...　…に就任する
garment　衣服、長い上着
ticker-tape parade　紙ふぶきの舞うパレード
poverty-stricken　とても貧乏な
tenement　借家、安アパート
immigration depot　移民収容所

predictably named Liberty Island. I cannot help preferring some of the other names that history tells us the tiny island bore over the centuries, including the appetizing Great Oyster Island and the poetic Love Island.

A Tea Drinker in a Coffee City

New York runs on coffee. People here drink it all the time. You see people buying morning lattes on the way to work, picking one up on the way back from lunch or finishing up an evening meal with an espresso. You see them sitting for hours at coffee shops, often working away on their computers.

I know of people who spend over a hundred dollars a month on coffee. They even use the terminology of drugs to describe coffee, talking about how expensive their coffee "habit" is or about getting their "fix" of coffee.

Coffee is available everywhere. Apparently

Vocabulary
run on...　…を燃料とする
work away　せっせと働き続ける
terminology　専門用語
fix　習慣になってやめられないもの

there are nearly 200 Starbucks within two miles of my office. I cannot even guess how high that number would rise if you include all the Dunkin' Donuts and bagel shops etc. that serve coffee.

On this matter I am totally out of place in New York. I only drink coffee occasionally and see it as far inferior to tea, the great British beverage. For all the thousands of coffee shops in New York, I have yet to find anywhere here that serves a better cup of tea than I can make at home for a fraction of the price.

Many coffee shops serve tea as though it is an afterthought. Usually they just dangle a teabag, of varying quality, in a paper cup of hot water. Sometimes if you order a large tea you just get the same tea bag and more hot water, which just means weaker tea. At some places the only tea they actually make for you is a sickly sweet chai latte.

I tried the famous Russian Tea Room in

Midtown, but it turned out to really be a restaurant. The tea was nothing special, though the decor was gorgeous. I tried Alice's Tea Cup on West 73rd Street which had the opposite problem: I liked the tea but disliked the decor (it is an Alice in Wonderland-themed café).

Let me explain the merits of tea over coffee. First, the taste. Taste is a personal matter but I would argue that tea is subtler and more distinguished. A pleasant Darjeeling has a complex taste that delights the tongue. It deserves its appellation "the champagne of teas". Earl Grey is perhaps the most refreshing tea. In the morning, when your taste buds are a little dull, I recommend English Breakfast. If it is foggy, rainy and cold you could opt for Irish Breakfast,

Vocabulary
out of place 場違いの
subtle 繊細な、ほのかな
distinguished 気品のある
taste bud 味覚
opt for... …を選ぶ

which is that little bit stronger and more fortifying. My latest favourite is Assam, which I had never drunk before this year—a testament to the variety of teas.

I really believe that if people had the opportunity to taste good tea many would not go back to coffee. (Coffee has one distinct advantage over tea: it smells better. It's a shame it doesn't taste as good as it smells.)

The second reason I prefer tea is that coffee really does act more like a drug (while tea is more like a refreshment). The caffeine content in coffee is far higher, and it seems stores now aim for a bigger dose. I particularly remember a couple of occasions when coffee in New York left me physically jittery and slightly anxious. (It is also a powerful diuretic.)

My third reason is difficult to explain, but it is closely linked to the first two. People drink coffee like it is fuel. It often seems joyless, like they just need to get it into them to help drive them along. A good cup of tea does just the opposite. It makes you slow down and appreciate the moment you are in. You don't need lots of expensive machinery to grind or steam. You can get a teapot and some decent leaf tea for a few dollars. Then you just need a little bit of time and patience.

I suspect the main reason New Yorkers don't drink much tea is that they think they can't spare the few minutes it takes tea to brew fully. Of course, the fact that they are busy is precisely why they should stop and enjoy the little rituals of making tea. Don't forget to warm the pot, one spoon of tea per cup and one extra "for the pot", always give it a stir before pouring...

Vocabulary
fortifying 元気を与える
testament to... …の証拠
dose （薬の）1服
jittery そわそわする、神経過敏な
diuretic 利尿剤

An Oasis in the City

As I write this it is "Labor Day", a national holiday that falls on the first Monday of September and unofficially signals the end of summer. Tomorrow, all the outdoor pools will be closed and children will be returning to school. I marked this day by visiting Central Park, where I have spent an enormous amount of time this summer observing people and investigating the park itself.

Central Park exists all year round of course but it really comes to life in summer. For much of the year it is too cold to wander around outside, but during the hot months the park is a hive of activity. Or should I say *activities*. On any given summer afternoon there will be people running, cycling, skating, swimming, boating, walking the dog, strolling, sunbathing, playing volleyball or throwing a Frisbee. There are lush green baseball fields but, this being Manhattan, there are no proper football (i.e. "soccer") fields and the game is only played in a couple of dusty spots at the edge of the park. There will be people eating, either at one of the three restaurants or at picnics. The picnickers are at a disadvantage: in New York you are not allowed to drink alcohol outside, though quite a lot of people secretly bring bottles of wine. There are also no barbecues allowed in Central Park, which is quite unusual for America.

There are lots of organized events. The New York Philharmonic Orchestra gave a free concert this summer, as did Bon Jovi. (I attended the former but skipped the latter.) Every day, people queued at the Delacorte Theatre in the

Vocabulary

Labor Day 労働者の日 [国民の祝日]
hive of activity 活動の中心地
lush （草木が）青々と生い茂った
i.e. すなわち [ラテン語の id est より]

park to see a production of *Hair*, a musical that is actually set in Central Park, if you follow me.

The park was designed by an energetic duo called Frederick Law Olmsted and Calvert Vaux back in 1857. Apparently, Olmsted was inspired by his visit in 1850 to Birkenhead Park in Liverpool, the first publicly funded park in England—another thing the Americans should thank the English for. Without Central Park, I think Manhattan would be unliveable. Whereas London has around ten major parks, Manhattan really has only one huge park and a few minor ones.

It's the perfect antidote to the concrete city it sits in. While the roads in Manhattan run rigidly north to south or east to west, the paths in the park twist and turn. It's quite possible to lose all sense of direction, which makes the park seem bigger than it is. It's big enough to change considerably in character as you move through it unlike, say, Yoyogi Park. The south, near Midtown, gets very crowded but the north is quiet, woody and shaded.

The park is a very social place. I often juggle with my football and usually within minutes someone asks to join in. Today I saw a group call over to a man with a guitar and ask him to play *Happy Birthday*.

Everyone has a favourite part of the park. Mine is Sheep Meadow, an open expanse of grass in the south of the park. Apparently there really were sheep on it until 1934. The meadow is lush and green but has pleasant views of the skyline. It is a designated "Quiet Zone", so no dogs, radios or bicycles are allowed, but other than that it can be fairly boisterous with American footballs being tossed and Frisbees sailing

Vocabulary
antidote 望ましくない状態を中和するもの
rigidly 厳密に
open expanse of grass 広々とした芝生
boisterous 騒がしい

at all angles. On a summer's evening you often get a choice of music: at one end you can hear the band playing in the garden of the famous Tavern on the Green restaurant, at the other end you are close to the Summer Stage where there are regular concerts.

The meadow might contain several thousand people on a nice day, but one rainy afternoon I was one of just a dozen or so people there. I remember how the sun broke through the clouds and a rainbow formed, rising from the ground just a few feet away from me and forming a perfect arch that ended at the far side of the meadow. I could hardly believe such an astounding act of nature could happen in the middle of a city.

I sometimes think it is called Central Park because it is so central to the city's well-being.

Vocabulary
well-being 幸福、安寧

Why "the Big Apple" Isn't "the Big Chestnut"

Ever since I first heard the term I have wondered why New York is called "the Big Apple". The city doesn't grow apples. The locals don't eat them in unusually large quantities. I have even stared at a map of the city, trying to see if it looks like an apple. (It doesn't.)

You see the term Big Apple everywhere, but no one seems to know where it comes from. When I ask people I usually get one of two answers: either "It's just a nickname for New York" or the only slightly more revealing "We call New York the Big Apple because it's big". Well, why not "the Big Chestnut" then?

Vocabulary
the Big Apple　ビッグアップル [NY市の愛称]

Fortunately, one man was as dissatisfied with these answers as me. Barry Popik trawled through ancient newspapers and documents in the New York public library to track down every use of the term and uncover its etymology. His research was very extensive, possibly obsessive, but his answer goes something like this: Horses like apples. So, decades ago, a big racetrack that hosted important meetings and gave valuable prizes might be referred to as a "big apple" in horseracing slang.

A horseracing reporter named John J. FitzGerald apparently first heard this term used by grooms in New Orleans in the 1920s. He liked it so much he titled his column in the *New York Morning Post* "Around the Big Apple".

In 1924 he took the trouble to explain it to his readers: "The Big Apple. The dream of every lad that ever threw a leg over a thoroughbred and the goal of all horsemen. There's only one Big Apple. That's New York."

In the 1930s, jazz musicians also began to refer to New York as *their* Big Apple, because Harlem was then the pinnacle of the jazz world where anyone of talent dreamed of performing and finding success.

It was only in the 1970s that the expression really reached the wider world when it was adopted by the New York tourist board (replacing the horribly unoriginal "Fun City") as New York's semi-official nickname. It was a clever piece of rebranding. At the time, New York was associated with crime, strikes and power failures. "The Big Apple" suggested a much more

Vocabulary

trawl （情報などを）広く集める
etymology 語源
groom 馬番
lad 少年、坊や [ここでは厩務員]
thoroughbred サラブレッド
pinnacle （成功・名声の）極み
rebranding イメージチェンジ
power failure 停電

wholesome image. In the years in between, however, the term had fallen into disuse and New Yorkers had forgotten what it meant.

Indeed several false theories circulated, as catalogued by Mr Popik. Some said New York was the Big Apple because so many desperate people sold apples from carts during the Great Depression (ah, but the term pre-existed the crash of 1929). Others said it was because of the famous apple tree planted in 1647 by Peter Stuyvesant, the last Dutch governor of the city, which survived for 220 years on the corner of 13th Street and 3rd Avenue (except that the history books show this was a *pear* tree).

It's difficult to be absolutely certain where any word or expression first came from. But in 1997 the mayor's office informally accepted Mr Popik's version of events when it added the name "Big Apple Corner" to the spot where Broadway meets West 54th Street. It was here that the long-forgotten racing reporter Mr

FitzGerald lived for the last 30 years of his life.

I can't think of any city with a more famous nickname. Only Rome, "the Eternal City"; Detroit, "Motor City"; New Orleans, "the Big Easy"; and Chicago, "the Windy City", come close. London or Tokyo, for example, don't really have descriptive names that are in common usage. (For the record, London is still sometimes called "the Big Smoke", because it was famous for chimney smoke and fog until the 1950s.)

New York, in fact, even has a few spare names including "the City that Never Sleeps", "the Empire City" and "Gotham". The first of these is self-explanatory, so I guess that just leaves the mystery of what the other two mean.

Vocabulary
wholesome 健全な
Gotham ゴッサム [昔、住民が皆愚かであったと伝わる英国中部のゴータム村より]
self-explanatory 自明の

Polish New York

One of the interesting aspects of living in New York is that you get to learn not just about America but about people of other nationalities. All kinds of immigrants live here, often in little enclaves where their native culture is preserved. In Greenpoint, an area of Brooklyn where I lived for several months, I learned a little bit about Poland.

Greenpoint lies just across the East River from 14th Street in Manhattan, but it's a very different place. It started as an industrial area, including the shipyards where the early "ironclads" were built, and still has many old industrial buildings and warehouses. These days it's more residential and many old buildings have been converted to shops, restaurants and apartments. A huge old water tower looms large over the waterfront area and, as if to symbolically claim the area, someone has painted a Polish flag on it.

For me, Greenpoint just doesn't quite seem like it's in New York. For one thing, it isn't well served by public transport so is quite isolated. It takes a surprisingly long time to get to Manhattan. Also, it is one of the few places in New York where the tallest building are the churches. This gives Greenpoint the feel of a village rather than a part of a city of skyscrapers. And then there are the Polish people, who make up nearly 50 percent of the local population.

Vocabulary
enclave （国・都市の中の）他民族集団の居住地
shipyard 造船所
ironclad 装甲艦
warehouse 倉庫
water tower 給水塔
loom （巨大なものが）そびえ立つ

Many stores have signs saying "Polish Spoken Here" (in Polish of course) and Polish is the language you hear most on the street. There are Polish restaurants, serving delicacies little known to most other people such as kielbasa (a kind of sausage). Pig's knuckles and various pickles are also part of the cuisine. There are numerous Polish bakeries, selling a variety of sweet confectionaries including kolacki ("stuffed" cookies). I noted, though, that the most popular tea in the Polish delis is not Polish but Twinings Tea from England—a sign of good taste.

The local bars and supermarkets all boast that they stock Polish beers, such as Tyskie and Zywiec. I liked the latter if only because of the strange combination of letters: z, y and w are among the rarer letters in the Roman alphabet. I can't think of any words in English that contain all three, let alone in succession. I learned that although Polish uses the same letters as

English this is of limited use in guessing pronunciation. Zywiec is pronounced something like jhiv-yets (the first letter is like the second g in garage).

At nearby McCarren Park you see lots of people playing football, which is quite rare in New York. Many of them wear shirts or shorts with the white eagle of Poland. I watched a Polish team play one afternoon and the goalkeeper was the best and most athletic I had ever seen in an amateur game. In fact, the Poles have a reputation for producing good goalkeepers. At the Euro 2008 tournament it was said jokingly that three of the best eleven Polish players were

Vocabulary
delicacy 珍味、ごちそう
pig's knuckle 豚のひざ肉

goalkeepers. Way back in 1973, a particularly stunning goalkeeping display by Jan Tomaszewski helped Poland to qualify for the World Cup Finals instead of England.

The Poles are well known in Europe for being churchgoing. Perhaps it's a coincidence but I was able to count six churches and one synagogue in the space of five blocks in the old part of Greenpoint.

The Polish have their own heroes. One is Pope John Paul II whose benign face you see on posters in shop windows. I was moved to find out the story of another priest, Father Jerzy Popieluszko. He never visited the US but a monument bearing his bust stands in Greenpoint. Popieluszko was murdered by secret police in Poland in 1984, aged 37, because he repeatedly and fearlessly denounced communism from the pulpit. His life and death helped strengthen the Solidarity movement that toppled communism. Local people lit candles at his statue to mark the anniversary of his death on October 19th.

For me, it was a strange thing to come to New York but end up inspired by the story of a Polish man.

Vocabulary
synagogue シナゴーグ
benign face 恩顔
denounce communism 共産主義を糾弾する
pulpit 説教壇
Solidarity 連帯［ポーランドの自主管理労組］
topple 打倒・転覆する

Emergency? Call 911
Fed Up? Call 311

Every country has its emergency services hotline. In England it's 999 and in America it's 911. So I was curious to hear people talking about dialling 311. Everyone in New York seemed to know what it was, but I hadn't a clue.

It turns out that 311 is a 24-hour hotline that operates for a range of non-emergency situations that can crop up at anytime and that the city government might be able to help with. I see it as a wonderful, empowering invention. After all, most people have far fewer life-threatening emergencies than they do quality of life issues.

In New York, 311 is called by around 50,000 people on an average weekday (or over 15 million calls a year). It is the best way to access local government services and to request information. You can call to report that a hole has appeared in your road (this happens surprisingly often in New York) or just to ask about how to separate your garbage.

But the most common reason to call is to make a complaint. People call to complain about a landlord who isn't fulfilling his end of a contract. (Landlords who fail to make repairs are a regular source of discontent in New York.) In winter, there are a lot of calls about failed heating systems. The city deals with these quickly because the nights can turn bitterly cold. Noise complaints happen all year but peak in summer when people play music with their windows

Vocabulary
fed up うんざり・いらいらして
crop up （問題などが）持ち上がる
empowering （人に）力を与える
landlord 家主
fulfill one's end of a contract 契約を履行する
discontent 不満、不平

open and when antiquated air conditioning units make a terrible racket.

The operators can give information about what the caller can do, can set things in motion so that city workers will do the necessary or can decide that the call is an emergency that needs to be passed to 911 operators.

Some other cities also have a 311 hotline, but New York's is the biggest. Chicago, for example, gets fewer than 4 million calls a year. And where else but New York can you expect to find a translation service available for over 170 languages?

But for me, 311 is not just an interesting idea. It's something that I have used—unlike 911, 999 or 110—and that I found effective and very satisfying.

In my case, the problem was noise. I live near a bar that plays loud, pounding music deep into the night, sometimes until 4 a.m., usually five nights a week. Once, I went inside to talk to the owner but the noise was too loud to hold a conversation, despite there being only around a dozen customers.

One night around 2 a.m., when a particularly noisy party was preventing me from sleeping, I decided to call 311. The operator patiently talked me through the procedures if I wanted to make a formal complaint. She referred me to a website page which outlined the rules on noise and explained that if I left my name and address a form would be sent to me and I could request someone to come to read the noise level in the apartment. She told me the bar could be warned or fined for violations of noise levels.

Vocabulary
antiquated 古い、老朽化した
racket 騒音
fined 罰金を科されて

I felt much better for knowing that there were steps I could take. The operator also immediately alerted my local police station about the noise complaint.

I didn't actually expect much would happen from one phone call. But I was wrong. The police visited the bar within an hour and the music was turned right down. The bar must have been in blatant violation of the rules because it was subsequently closed down for several weeks. It was a blissful relief and every night I said a silent thank you to 311.

Vocabulary
blatant violation 露骨な違反
subsequently その後
blissful 至福の

Why Is Everyone Being So Nice to Me?

Before I ever set foot in America I was certain of one thing: New Yorkers are rude. They argue constantly and loudly. They look down their noses at you. They will rob you and cheat you given half a chance. It is a city where you need to be aggressive just to get by.

There is a film, called *The Out-of-Towners*, which is about this exact subject. A married couple arrive in New York and, over the course of one horrible day, suffer ever possible indignity: mugging, strikes, cancelled reservations... Personally, though, I remembered the scene in *Crocodile Dundee* when he arrives in New York and keeps trying to introduce himself to people

Vocabulary
get by　なんとかやっていく
suffer indignity　侮辱・冷遇される
mugging　強盗

in the street, as they hurry past. "That's New York," I thought.

Except that when I actually arrived in New York everyone seemed to be on their best behaviour. People I didn't know would smile at me. I was called "sir" more times within the first few days here than in my whole life up to that point. Staff in shops would enquire about what kind of day I was having and heartily wish me a "great evening" as I left.

Naturally, I was suspicious and tried to figure it out in my head. It couldn't be that I had somehow managed only to interact with the small number of New Yorkers for whom manners are important. With each friendly interaction that possibility became increasingly mathematically unlikely. Nor could I kid myself that I had somehow won over an otherwise hostile city with my good looks and English charm. (If only because I am neither good-looking nor charming.)

Finally, I decided I had the answer: it was all a trick. People were pretending to be nice with the intention of lulling me into a false sense of security. The girl smiling at me in the park was no doubt hoping to "borrow" ten dollars from me if I responded. The taxi driver who asked me was it my first time in New York was hoping that I would be stupid enough to say "yes", so that he could take me the long way around and charge me for it. The people in the shops weren't actually planning a crime but they were being falsely nice in an effort to trick me into spending all my money in their shop.

I reacted accordingly. I would walk around town with a purposeful stride intended to indicate that I was no tourist. In Central Park, which I had heard was particularly dangerous,

Vocabulary
enquire = inquire 尋ねる
lull one into... だまして…の状態にする

I would adopt a facial expression that (I hoped) would show I was streetwise and tough. When people smiled at me I would just nod as if to say: "I know what you're up to and you're not fooling me."

I look back at that period of my life now and laugh. The obvious reason people seemed to be being unnaturally nice to me was just that people in New York, on the whole, are very friendly and polite. People say "bless you" if you sneeze on the subway. In elevators, where people normally go completely and uncomfortably silent, New Yorkers exchange pleasantries. I have seen people get angry in Post Offices and shops, but far more often the customers and staff chat like old friends. Today, for example, I went to buy milk and the store owner wanted to talk to me about what the papers were saying about President Obama. And the doorman of the building where I live has started greeting me by my first name. (There must be over a thousand residents. How does he remember?)

I would say that New Yorkers are far more friendly than people from Tokyo or London, the two other cities I know best. A Swiss friend recently told me she was shocked that someone stopped to show her how to operate a payphone when she first came to New York.

Of course, there are exceptions. Even nice New Yorkers seem to undergo a terrible character change when they get into their cars. And when they argue, people are so absolutely sure they are definitely in the right, even when they are not, which is infuriating. But, on the whole, the reputation of New Yorkers as unfriendly and combative is based mainly on the fact that

Vocabulary
streetwise 世慣れた
pleasantry あいさつ、冗談
infuriating 腹立たしい
combative けんか好きな

across whole swathes of America people are *even more* friendly. In the Midwest, from my limited knowledge of it, people walk around smiling and greeting each other constantly.

Indeed, there are times when I find it all a bit much. At certain shops (Trader Joe's the supermarket, for example) the friendliness is a bit overwhelming and I yearn for the anonymity and privacy of England or Japan. I wonder if the chirpy American shop assistant really wants to know how my day has been? I once formulated a plan to reply that my cat has died and my income is collapsing. But then I couldn't actually deliver the line. After all, everyone is being so nice it would be rude of me to ruin it.

Vocabulary
across whole swathes of America アメリカ全土にわたって
yearn for the anonymity 匿名性を懐かしく思う
chirpy 陽気な
deliver the line その文を声に出して言う

The Oxford – New York Dictionary, Part One

A collection of words and terms that occur often in New York and almost never in England:

Bridezilla (noun)
A woman who undergoes monstrous character change when planning her wedding, becoming aggressive, controlling and demanding. Combines the word "bride" with the word "Godzilla". Sample sentence: "When she heard Donna Karan wouldn't personally design her wedding dress she had a Bridezilla moment."

Chutzpah (noun)
From Yiddish, meaning self-confidence, shamelessness or nerve. Usually used in a negative

Vocabulary ————————————————
Yiddish イディッシュ [ドイツ語にスラブ語・ヘブライ語を交えた言語]

sense, but sometimes positive. One of many Jewish words used by English speakers in New York. (See also kvetch, schlep, schmuck.)
Sample sentence: "Illinois governor Rod Blagojevich sure has some chutzpah, turning up for interview on the David Letterman show after being impeached for trying to sell a Senate seat."

Funky (adjective)

In addition to the widely used positive meaning (cool, enjoyable, groovy), can also mean unpleasant, particularly in relation to smells, depending on context.
Sample sentence: "There's a funky smell in your fridge."

Hipster (noun)

Trendy middle-class youth, usually in urban areas. Despite the association with the positive word "hip", hipster is generally used in a derogatory manner to refer to fashionable but soulless young people. Hipsters are accused of adopting—rather than creating—fashions and movements. Current New York hipster fashion includes tattooing and drinking Pabst Blue Ribbon beer, both adopted from working-class culture.

Sample sentence: "Williamsburg used to be interesting but now it's just full of hipsters."

Octomom (noun)

Used especially in the media to refer to Nadya Suleman, who gave birth to eight live babies in California in 2009 after undergoing IVF.

Sample headline: Octomom Already Had Six Kids

Vocabulary

impeached 告発・弾劾されて
Senate seat 上院の議席
derogatory 軽蔑的な
soulless 空っぽな、つまらない
IVF = in vitro fertilization 体外受精

Perp Walk (noun, slang)
Abbreviated from "perpetrator's walk", when police intentionally or coincidentally parade a person under arrest before the press. The perp walk typically occurs when the accused is moved from police station to police vehicle ahead of a court appearance. The accused is usually handcuffed and clearly under the restraint of police officers.

Sample sentence: "Have you noticed how they always do a big perp walk when a politician gets arrested?"

Pied-a-terrè (noun)
From French, meaning a small apartment in the city, separate from one's main residence, which a wealthy person maintains for convenience.

Pinkertons (noun)
A private detective agency famous in the US in the 19th century. The Pinkertons were often

employed in lawless regions as bodyguards or to track down fugitives. Regularly referenced in period dramas and today used occasionally in an ironic manner.
Sample sentence: "If he doesn't pay me back that $50 soon I'll get the Pinkertons onto him."

Pinky (noun)
American-English meaning the little finger on each hand.

Shower (noun)
A gathering, as in "baby shower" or "bridal shower", that precedes the event it celebrates as an expression of support. At a baby shower female friends might give advice and offers of

Vocabulary
perpetrator 犯人、犯罪者
the accused 被告人
under the restraint of... …に拘束されて
track down fugitive 逃亡者を追い詰める

help to a pregnant woman and bring gifts for the baby. Men are not usually invited.

Sic (transitive verb)
To order an attack, particularly by dogs.
Sample sentence: "If you come any closer I'll sic my dog on you."

Two Buck Chuck (noun, slang)
Widely used nickname for the exceptionally cheap wine produced by the company Charles Shaw (Chuck being short for Charles). Particularly popular with students and associated with the supermarket Trader Joe's. In New York the price is now typically $3, and it is therefore sometimes called Three Buck Chuck.
Sample sentence: "I got drunk on Two Buck Chuck last night and feel awful."

Vocabulary
buck　1ドル [dollar の口語]

The Oxford – New York Dictionary, Part Two

Brownstone (noun)

A type of house common in New York, usually dating from the late 19th and early 20th century. The name derives from the distinctive building material. The typical brownstone is terraced and is four or five storeys, including the basement. Brownstones might have originally housed one family but most are now converted so that each floor is one apartment.

Sample sentence: "My ambition is to own a whole brownstone."

Chick flick (noun)

A film that is primarily of interest to women, usually by design. (See also "chick lit".)

Sample sentence: *"Sex and the City* is the ulti-

Vocabulary
by design 故意・計画的に

mate chick flick."

Diner dash (noun)
To leave a restaurant without paying the bill.
Sample sentence: "I only ever did a diner dash once, when I was a student."

Dumpster diver (noun)
A person who searches through garbage for useable items. Particularly used in reference to people who retrieve food from dumpsters outside supermarkets.
Sample sentence: "In the recession the number of dumpster divers is increasing. They say a lot of discarded food is perfectly edible, just that the supermarket has to throw it once it reaches its sell-by date."

Joe, cup o' / cuppa (noun)
Coffee, particularly regular coffee rather than more sophisticated versions such as caffè latte.

The origin of the word is uncertain but may derive from "Java", the coffee-growing region of Indonesia.

Sample sentence: "Nothing wakes me up in the morning like a cup o' Joe."

No-brainer (noun)

A choice or decision so simple that it requires little or no thought.

Sample sentence: "Do I want to pay $20 for a salad at the health food place or go for the $25 buffet down the block? Well, that's a no-brainer."

Schlep (verb)

To carry or drag, usually with some effort. From Yiddish. Sometimes used reflexively as in "to schlep oneself".

Vocabulary
dumpster　大型ゴミ容器
retrieve...from~　…を〜から回収する
recession　不況
discarded　捨てられた

Sample sentence: "I had to schlep two suitcases across the city by subway."

Schwinned (passive verb)
To be hit by a bicycle. The word derives from Schwinn, a bicycle manufacturer.
Sample sentence: "I like visiting college towns, but you are always getting schwinned."

Stoop (noun)
The steps leading up to a house. Particularly common in "brownstone" buildings.
Sample sentence: "Did you see in the papers about the 'Brooklyn beer man' getting fined by the police for drinking on his own stoop?"

Straphanger (noun)
A commuter or other regular user of public transport. So called because standing passengers often grip straps for stability on trains and buses.
Sample sentence: "Straphangers in New York

are up in arms over plans to raise prices on the subway by a whopping 25 percent."

Suds (noun, slang)

Beer, particularly cheap, gassy beer that produces a lot of bubbles.
Sample sentence: "Sounds like you've had a hard day. What you need is some suds."

Walk-up (noun)

An apartment building where there is no elevator, so you are required to "walk up" the stairs. In a country famed for its aversion to physical effort, this is considered a drawback.
Sample sentence: "My friend lives on the top of a five-storey walk-up. It's fine until you have loads of shopping."

Vocabulary
up in arms　憤慨して
whopping　べらぼうな
suds　ビール（の泡）
aversion　避けたい気持ち

Historical Titbits About New York

Winston Churchill was half-American...

and possibly one-sixteenth Native American. Churchill's mother was a New Yorker, born at 197 Amity Street, Brooklyn. It's ironic that the man often called "the greatest ever Englishman" was actually half-American. His mother, Jennie Jerome, was the daughter of a wealthy New York financier. In 1953, while serving as prime minister, Churchill visited Brooklyn to see the house where his mother was born. But it is believed now that he was taken to the wrong house: he was shown a house on nearby Henry Street, where his grandparents had lived briefly with his great-uncle.

Jennie Jerome believed all her life that her grandmother was the daughter of an Iroquois Indian. Though the historical evidence suggests this may be untrue, it is "family lore", believed in turn by Winston Churchill and members of his family today.

New York gave chewing gum to the world

A New Yorker, Thomas Adams, was the "inventor" of chewing gum. While experimenting to find an industrial use for chicle, a gum extracted from trees, he popped some in his mouth and realised it was good to chew. Adams, who lived and died in Brooklyn, was the first to mass-produce "snapping and stretching gum", as he called it, and he patented a machine to manufacture gum in 1871. He was also the first to sell it from vending machines, which appeared in New York subway stations in 1888.

Vocabulary
titbit = tidbit とっておきの・おもしろい小話
family lore 家訓
snap パチンと音をさせる
patent 独自に開発する、専売特許とする

Townshend Harris created New York's first free university

Before heading to Japan in 1856 to become the US' first diplomat there, Harris was the president of the Board of Education in New York City. He is honoured as the founder of the first free public institution of higher education in the US in 1847. Today, the school he founded is called City College of New York. "Open the doors to all," declared Harris. "Let the children of the rich and the poor take their seats together and know of no distinction save that of industry, good conduct and intellect." Harris is buried in Green-Wood Cemetery in Brooklyn, where his grave is marked with a *toro* lantern from Shimoda and a plaque from City College.

Central Park had an English inspiration

Both Central Park in Manhattan and Prospect Park in Brooklyn were built by the same duo, Calvert Vaux and Frederick Law Olmsted, over 15 years starting in 1858. Both parks are rightly considered wonderful examples of the American tradition of city parks. But it is less well-known that this tradition owes a debt to the English. Vaux was himself from England, while Olmsted was greatly inspired in his plan for Central Park by a visit to Liverpool's Birkenhead Park, during a trip to England in 1850. Olmsted was impressed not only by the landscaping of Birkenhead Park, by the great British designer Joseph Paxton, but also the concept of a public park, which had not yet reached the US. He noted the irony that in "democratic" America there was no equivalent of this "People's Park", publicly funded, run by local government and open to all.

Vocabulary

diplomat 外交官
institution 教育機関
save... …を除外する [ここでは except と同義]
plaque 小板状の飾り
no equivalent of... …に相当するものはない

Ticker-tape statistics

A unique New York institution is the ticker-tape parade, which proceeds along lower Broadway. There have been 165 parades since the first in 1886 to celebrate the dedication of the Statue of Liberty. The parades are normally held for visiting foreign dignitaries (popes, kings and prime ministers), soldiers, sporting champions, and aviators and spacemen. The longest gap between parades lasted nine years, from 1910 to 1919, but then there were three in three months. There were nine parades in 1951 and nine in 1962. In 1951, among those honoured were Douglas MacArthur, returning from Occupied Japan, and Sir Denys Lowson, a mostly forgotten and little-admired figure who was once Lord Mayor of London. Today, parades seem to be falling out of favour: there have been only two since 2000. The aviator Richard Evelyn Byrd is the only man to have had three parades. Six Frenchmen and six Britons have had parades in their honour, but the French "win" because Charles de Gaulle had two parades. And you could also say the parade for the Statue of Liberty was a kind of honour for the French because they built it, thus sparking off the whole tradition.

Vocabulary
aviator 飛行士
fall out of favour 人気がなくなる
sparking off 引き起こす

How I Became "Litigious"

"America is a very litigious society." I remember reading that in a newspaper when I was a teenager. I remember it because I had to get a dictionary and look up the word "litigious", although it was clear from the story that it was something bad. It means "inclined to take disputes to court", or "excessively ready to resort to legal action". I think the story was something about silly Americans burning their mouths by drinking coffee before it had cooled down, then suing restaurants for damages.

Well, now I have first-hand experience of this "litigious society" because I have recently been to court for the first time in my life.

When I left an apartment I had been renting, the landlady was supposed to return the security deposit of $1,300 to me within a month. One month passed, then another without any contact from her. I emailed her and left phone messages, before it slowly became apparent to me that she intended to keep the money.

Obviously, this is entirely against the law. But I did a little bit of research and found that it is a fairly common problem in New York. It seems sneaky landlords try to do this because tenants may lack the resources to do anything about it. (They either don't know how to pursue the money or cannot because, for example, they are from another country and have gone back.) People sometimes just give up on the money because it seems like a lot of trouble to get it back.

Vocabulary
litigious 訴訟好きな
take disputes to court 法廷で争う
resort to legal action 法的措置をとる
sue 訴訟を起こす
first-hand 直接体験によって得た
security deposit 敷金
lack the resources to... …するための資力がない

Fortunately, I have a friend who is a lawyer and he encouraged me to do something, giving me plenty of advice and help. We wrote letters to the landlady asking for the return of the money and sent them by registered post. Her only reply was a phone call to my friend in which she announced that she was keeping the money because I had wrecked the apartment. This was a horrible lie and it made me more determined to go to court.

We gathered letters of reference from previous landlords, who kindly wrote that I had been a good tenant. Then I filed a court action at the Small Claims Court in Brooklyn. I paid $20 to start the case and then had to wait around six weeks for my day in court.

I was nervous about appearing in court and didn't sleep much the night before. I printed out a list of all the points I wanted to make and brought with me copies of the contract, the letters we sent her and the references. But

I needn't have been so worried. The arbitrator (a kind of judge) was very helpful, expertly guiding me to establish the two important points: that the landlady had not done as agreed in the contract and had not followed the correct procedure for withholding the deposit.

The landlady didn't even come to the court to explain herself. So the arbitrator awarded me the full $1,300 plus an extra $100 to cover my costs. It was a very happy moment for me.

I have told this to a few friends from England and Japan, and most of them shook their heads in disgust at the landlady. They felt it was sadly typical of America that someone would try to cheat me like that. I agree that

Vocabulary
registered post 書留郵便
wreck 破壊・破損する
letter of reference 推薦状、紹介状
file a court action 裁判所に告訴状を提出する
contract 契約書

the landlady is a bad person, but I also felt very grateful that it was so simple and cheap to bring a court case to recover the lost money. My lawyer friend helped me, but I really could have done it by myself. I was amazed and impressed that the court would provide interpreters free of charge for people who didn't speak English. Not just Spanish and Chinese interpreters, any language. There are also volunteer lawyers to help you prepare your case if you need.

When I was living in Japan many years ago I twice lost money when landlords took a very large portion of my deposit to use to redecorate the apartments. (In fact, tenants are only supposed to pay for damage beyond "normal wear and tear".) On those occasions I felt really cheated but I didn't know how to fight against it. Now, there is a small claims system in Japan. But there wasn't at that time, nor did anyone suggest to me that I could take legal action. Japan isn't "litigious" like that.

So now when I hear the term "litigious society" it doesn't only have a negative meaning. It can also mean a place where it is possible to get justice.

Vocabulary
normal wear and tear　経年による消耗や傷み

Treasure Hunting in Brooklyn

When I make tea, I always use a made-in-England teapot because the tea brews to a richer flavour. I drink it from an attractive Chinese mug with a lid, which helps to keep it hot if I take long pauses between sips. When I drink red wine, I like to pour it first into a decanter which allows the wine to breathe for a while and allows me to admire its colour. With beer, I usually drink from a ceramic cup with a handle, because this stops the beer from warming up in my hand. As I drink, I might gaze at a beautiful framed print of Edward Hopper's painting *Early Sunday Morning*. Or I might glance at my mirror which bears a picture of a train and the words "Union Pacific Railway".

I mention these things partly because I love them, in so far as one can feel love for a physical object, but also because I found all of them on the street, left there by someone to be picked up.

It's something I never expected in New York, but in this supposedly "throwaway society" there is a tradition of "recycling" goods. Things are put out neatly in front of the house or apartment block, sometimes with a little note that might say "this works" if it is a piece of electronic equipment. Usually, it is left out the day before rubbish collection so that if no-one claims it, it can be carted off by the garbage men.

You don't see this all across the city. In fact, 90 percent of everything I have found was in Park Slope—a middle-class neighbourhood of Brooklyn that has a strong environmental ethos. This happens to be where I live now, and

Vocabulary
brew （茶が）はいる
ethos 気風、エートス

it's a particularly nice area to go for a walk. So I often go out empty-handed for a stroll and return with an armful of treasure.

I found a few bits and pieces in Williamsburg, but since this is a "younger" area the things left out tended to be bits of crockery and second-hand clothes. In Park Slope, there is not just a lot of stuff put out, it tends to be of good quality. I have an excellent collection of books that I found. To mention a few, Albert Camus' *The Plague* which I am enjoying right now; the autobiography of the former geisha Mineko Iwasaki (I interviewed her in Kyoto many years ago and remember many of her stories); an account of the battle of Okinawa; *Bright Lights, Big City* (one of the classic novels of New York) and a collection of plays by Irish playwrights. The people of Park Slope have fairly highbrow tastes.

I really wish I had a record player because many people are dumping their record collections. I would love to take them all, and give each record a spin to see if I liked it. Who knows what wondrous sound I might discover? Even without a record player there were some records I just had to take. One day I will find a way to listen to Rudi Knabl ("Germany's Incredible King of the Zither") and the Aram Arakelian Ensemble's album *The Oud*.

This hobby gives me insight into people's lives and tastes. I have learned for example that women get rid of clothes that are still in good condition. Men don't. (I have found women's boots as good as new, but men only tend to put out old misshapen T-shirts.) I also discovered

Vocabulary
crockery 陶器類
playwright 劇作家、脚本家
highbrow 知的な、教養のある
insight 洞察
misshapen ゆがんだ

that there are a lot of children—and children's parties—in Park Slope, because I am always finding packets of balloons and children's books (along with such titles as *A Guide to Pregnancy* and *Childcare 101*). This makes sense because Park Slope is where New York couples often move when they have children.

When I came to New York I promised myself that I wouldn't accumulate much stuff, because it's so much trouble to take it with me when, eventually, I leave. But somehow it's easier to throw stuff away when I didn't pay for it in the first place. And easier still to put it back out onto the street where it might be picked up by someone who will love it as much as I did.

Vocabulary
accumulate ためる

The Uninsured Life

Recently I had the strange and slightly embarrassing experience of appealing for financial help.

I had been feeling a bit unwell (nothing serious, I should add) and wanted to visit a doctor. The problem was that my insurance had lapsed several months before and I had not renewed it. Medical care in the US is run as a private business and can be very expensive, so I was a bit concerned about the potential cost of a medical bill. When I explained at the medical centre that I neither had insurance nor a salaried job, I was told that I might qualify for cheaper treatment. I filled in a simple form stating my income (and some other circumstances) and

Vocabulary
uninsured 無保険の
lapse 失効する

was told that at that particular centre I was eligible for a reduction of around 50 percent.

It was, I suppose, a good result. I am almost never sick, but I know now that if I do have a simple problem I can get seen by a doctor relatively cheaply. The one time I did become badly ill, as it happens, was in New York in 2000 when I developed appendicitis. I was insured at the time, but I remember the doctor mentioning to me that hospitals were obliged to treat life-threatening illnesses regardless of the patient's ability to pay. And in the event that I developed a chronic illness, I would have the option of returning to my home country, the UK, where we have a National Health Service which is effectively free to users. (It is paid for from general taxation.)

So it seems I am covered for most scenarios, but only because I am lucky enough to live near a hospital with a charitable character and because I am British and have an "escape hatch".

It's well known that tens of millions of Americans do not have any kind of insurance—and that President Obama is attempting to create a universal healthcare system for the country. Anyone who has seen the film *Sicko*, by Michael Moore, may also be aware that even people who are insured may find the insurance company attempts to wriggle out of paying for their treatment. So I am not making a very original comment when I say that I think that healthcare in the US is an expensive mess, and is one of the clear drawbacks to being an American.

Americans have four main options for health insurance. The first is to find a secure job and hold on to it. Most people I know are covered by health insurance provided by their

Vocabulary
eligible for a reduction of...　…の割引資格がある
appendicitis　虫垂炎
chronic illness　慢性疾患
escape hatch　回避手段
wriggle out of paying　支払いをごまかす

employers. And most of those people are terrified of losing their jobs because they would also lose their insurance. (As one man put it to me recently: "Lose your job and you could lose your life.") The second option is to take a private insurance plan. Some self-employed people I know do this. The problem is that it is quite expensive and even then there is often what is called a "deductible". That is, people still have to pay their own medical bills unless the treatment is expensive (say, more than $1,000), at which point the insurance comes into effect. The third option is to apply for one of the government-funded health insurers, such as Medicaid (for the poor) and Medicare (for the elderly), but many poor people do not qualify. The fourth option is surprisingly common: to have no healthcare insurance at all. Emergency Rooms in hospitals will give treatment regardless of the ability to pay, so many uninsured people simply turn up there and wait (often for many hours).

This is far from ideal; most of those patients could have been treated far more effectively and far more cheaply had they been able to see a doctor before they got seriously unwell.

What struck me is how much fear and worry is caused by illness and healthcare in America—including to me. This is generally a very optimistic nation. Yet people here worry not just about getting sick, but about not being able to get the treatment they need if they do get sick. In 1941, President Roosevelt outlined what he called the "Four Freedoms" that he believed all people were entitled to. Alongside freedom of speech and freedom of religion, he included freedom from want. I cannot help feeling that, 70 years on, his country is failing to deliver in at least one regard.

Vocabulary
put it 述べる
deductible 控除免責金額 [被保険者の負担になる金額]
entitled 資格・権利の与えられた
regard 事項、細目

Some of My Least Favourite Americanisms

There are plenty of Americanisms that I like. Some are inventive, some are very evocative. But there are also some that I dislike—and a few that really irritate me. Sometimes I can't even explain why I dislike an expression. Maybe I'm just not being tolerant enough. After all, there are plenty of irritating British English expressions. Nevertheless, I am listing some of the expressions I hear in New York that I really don't like.

Are you still working on that?

This is how a waitress typically asks if you have finished your meal and whether she should take your plate away. I think I dislike it because it implies that eating is a task to be "worked on". Certainly, servings tend to be so large in America that finishing the whole plate is indeed a challenge, and this is one reason why the waitress has to check whether you have finished eating even if the plate is half full.

No, I'm done

A fairly common reply to the above question. It just sounds too casual and dismissive.

I could care less

The British version is "I couldn't care less", meaning "I don't care at all". Somehow the Americans dropped the "not" from the sentence, which should of course change the meaning. Except that the Americans use it to mean the same thing.

Vocabulary
Americanism アメリカ英語特有の語、米語
evocative 呼び起こす、喚起する
servings （飲食物の）1盛り、1杯
dismissive そっけない

I don't *give* a damn

We use the exact same words in England to mean "I don't care at all". But the Americans almost invariably emphasise the word "give", which is unnatural. Normally, you should stress the word "damn". There is an unusual story behind this. In the classic film *Gone with the Wind*, the male lead says these words at a pivotal moment in the story. (In fact, "Frankly, my dear, I don't *give* a damn" is possibly the single most famous line from any film.) However, in 1939 the word "damn" was considered a terrible curse word. So the actor Clark Gable chose to stress the word "give" when saying his line, to soften the impact of the word "damn". Americans have been doing so ever since.

We owned you

This expression is usually used in reference to sports or other competitive situations and means something like "we were much better than you" or "we completely dominated". I find it ugly to suggest "ownership" of another person, even if it is not meant literally.

My bad

Meaning "my fault", this just replaces a noun with an adjective. And it sounds wrong.

I feel you

A slightly creepy expression meaning "I understand your position".

Vocabulary

invariably つねに、必ず
lead 主役
pivotal moment きわめて重要な場面
curse word 不敬の言葉
creepy いやな感じのする

Whatever

This is used to mean "I don't care what you think" or even "I'm not listening to you". To be fair, it is also cited by Americans themselves as one of the most annoying expressions in their language.

Comfort station

In English we have a long tradition of euphemisms for "toilet". In England, we often say "bathroom" and in America they often say "restroom". But recently I discovered they also use the absurd term "comfort station" to mean public lavatory. (I considered it particularly unfortunate because that is also the English expression for the military brothels run by the Japanese in World War II.)

Happy Holidays

A greeting quite often used at Christmastime instead of "Happy Christmas", in case the person addressed is not Christian. The expression doesn't personally bother me that much. But a lot of English people find it maddeningly "politically correct" to ignore the fact that the holidays mark Christmas out of concern that a non-Christian might be offended.

Vocabulary
cite 引き合いに出す
euphemism 婉曲語法
absurd ばかげた
brothel 売春宿
politically correct 差別・偏見を排除しようとした
offended 不快に思って

Some of My Favourite Americanisms

It's an interesting experience to hear someone speaking the same language as you but using an expression you have never heard. Many of my favourite Americanisms may just be standard expressions to an American. But to me, they can be very funny or clever or useful. Here are a few favourites that I have heard since coming to New York:

Kicked to the kerb

An expression used to mean someone has been "dumped" by a boyfriend or girlfriend. It compares the experience to the way people might kick a piece of trash to the side of the street as they walk, thus vividly capturing the sense of how casually brutal it can feel when someone breaks up with you.

Smitten kitten

People are often said to be "smitten" by love. To call someone who has fallen deeply in love "a smitten kitten" accurately describes how cute and needy they appear. And the words rhyme too.

Bucket list

A "bucket list" is the list of things a person decides they want to do before they die, especially if they believe they are nearing the end of their lives. Derived from the old expression "to kick the bucket" which means "to die". The expression reminds me how practical and "goal-oriented" Americans are.

Vocabulary

kerb （歩道の）縁石
smitten うっとりした、夢中の
needy 愛情を強く欲している様子の
kick the bucket 死ぬ、くたばる

The walk of shame

When a person (usually a woman) has to return home in the early morning wearing the gaudy clothes from a night out. This usually signifies that she has gone out to a bar and unexpectedly stayed the night at someone else's apartment (i.e. a man's apartment).

Mad money

A small amount a woman keeps with her for emergencies. For example, a $50 note stashed in a pocket of her handbag so that she can get a taxi home if she has an argument (i.e. becomes "mad" or angry) with her boyfriend on a date.

Brodeo

When the people at a party or bar are almost entirely male. Usually used to express disappointment that there are not enough women. Derived from the words "bro", short for "brother", and "rodeo".

Thank you for sharing

This is an expression often used in American schools to praise a child for contributing to a class. But it can also be used sarcastically when, for example, an adult says something inappropriate such as telling friends at dinner about his recent medical procedure. If used gently, saying "thank you for sharing" can help defuse such awkward situations.

Keep telling yourself that

Another expression that can be used with gentle sarcasm between friends. If a friend is deluding himself by, for example, saying that he looks good even though he has put on a lot of weight, saying "keep telling yourself that"

Vocabulary
gaudy けばけばしい
stash そっとしまっておく
rodeo ロデオ［カウボーイの腕前を競う会］
defuse （緊張を）和らげる
delude oneself 自分自身を欺く

will indicate that he is wrong.

Yank someone's chain

Just as a dog gets annoyed if you pull the chain which goes around his neck, "to yank someone's chain" means to tease or annoy him deliberately. It's a pretty good comparison because people, just like dogs, are often quite easy to make angry.

Mystery meat

When meat has been prepared in such a way or cooked for so long that it is difficult to be sure from appearance or taste whether it is chicken, pork or beef. This kind of "mystery meat" might be found in pies, piroshkis or many dishes served in school canteens.

Vocabulary
yank... …をぐいと引っ張る
deliberately わざと
canteen (工場・学校の) 大食堂

The Great Sunday Times Reading Challenge

"How many sections are you fluent in?" This is the question posed in an advertisement for the *New York Times*' Sunday edition.

It's a fair question because the newspaper on Sundays is huge, diverse and challenging. It contains a whopping number of separate sections and typically weighs close to two kilograms. Personally, I think the Sunday *New York Times* is one of the city's great cultural achievements. It costs $5, which is quite expensive, but if you consider the number of experts who work to put it together it's still a bargain. A lot of people agree with me; over 1.4 million buy the Sunday paper, about 400,000 more than buy the daily paper.

I don't get the paper delivered but rather buy it on the way to the park. So my first goal is to reduce the weight by dumping all the parts

I don't want. (I don't think anybody reads the whole paper.) First to go is the Automobiles section (because I don't drive), then all the detachable advertisements and the Real Estate listings (because I could never buy a house in New York). Once a month there is a style magazine and occasionally a sport magazine. Both of these are heavy and not all that interesting so I usually dump them too.

Even so, there is still a lot of newspaper left by the time I reach the park. You would expect a person to start by reading the section that interests him most. I do the opposite because I am still trying to reduce the amount of paper I am carrying. I can usually skim through the Sports section in about five minutes because it focuses on sports that don't interest me much (baseball, American football, basketball...). The Business section doesn't take much longer because I am not fascinated by the world of finance and industry. It is rare that I spend much time on the

Travel section.

At this stage my progress through this mighty paper begins to slow. I always *think* I can skim through the Arts and Leisure section in a few minutes but I always seem to find one or two stories that I have to read from start to end, about a new exhibition at MOMA or a rare opera production at the Met. (It's a hallmark of a great paper that you end up reading with fascination about things you didn't expect to be interested in.)

Around this time I usually move to the main newspaper, with all the national and international stories. The newsroom at the *New York Times* is the heart of a newspaper widely considered to be the world's best. I admire the

Vocabulary
detachable advertisement 取り外しできる広告
real estate 不動産
skim through... …をざっと読む
hallmark 品質 (優良) 証明

thoroughness of the reporting, but I also find the stories a bit laborious. A *Times* story might be over 2,000 words, starting on one page and finishing on another. British newspapers tend to break the stories down into more manageable chunks of around 700 words. British papers also usually have punchier headlines, snazzier layouts and better pictures. (People call the *Times* "the old grey lady" because it's a bit staid.)

The Book Review is my favourite *section* of the paper. The reviews are intelligent and readable and the selection of books covered really matches my interests. However, my favourite single weekly *article* is called The Hunt, in which is described someone's search for their perfect apartment in New York. It's a very human story because you learn about the people as you hear their reasons for wanting to move out of one place in one part of town and into another, whether the reason be financial, social, practical or whatever.

Around this time I usually skip to the magazine. This is the most expensively produced part of the paper, with glossy pictures and top writers, so it tends to have the choicest stories. I might read one of the long articles or skip through a few of the shorter ones.

The problem is that I can never get through the whole paper in a day. Quite a lot of it goes into my bag to be read later in the week and so I often don't buy the daily paper. And that is the reason I am grateful for one more Sunday section: The Week in Review, which covers some of the stories I missed.

Vocabulary
laborious 長たらしい
snazzy しゃれた
staid 落ち着いた、まじめな
glossy 光沢紙を用いた
choicest 極上の

Damn You, Seinfeld

You can learn the local slang. You can blend in with how people dress. You can observe the customs, the taboos and the social norms. But living abroad there are still times when you are caught out by shared cultural references.

In New York, I am cursed by my ignorance of the comedy series *Seinfeld*, which ran for nine years and ended in 1998. It's a moderately funny show about the lives of four New Yorkers, centred on the main character a comedian named Jerry Seinfeld.

When I first visited New York in 1997 it was a must-see programme. People would rush home to catch each episode and you would be at a disadvantage the next day if you could not discuss the latest antics of "crazy" Kramer and Elaine, or the latest silly argument between George and Jerry.

So I knew *Seinfeld* was massively popular. But I didn't expect that over a decade later people would still be quoting it and making references to it. People will say laughingly: "That's the East River. Kramer went swimming in it!" or make jokes about a "puffy shirt", whatever that means. Most people my age and older in New York can remember almost every episode. Whereas I have only seen a few of them—and tend to forget them soon afterwards.

People will say, for example, "It's just like *The Chinese Restaurant*". (This refers to an episode of *Seinfeld* when three of the friends wait endlessly for a table at a restaurant.) Or they might say someone reminds them of "the Soup

Vocabulary
Seinfeld 『となりのサインフェルド』[NYを舞台にしたアメリカの国民的ドラマ]
social norm 社会的規範
caught out ボロが出て
be cursed by... …に呪われる・たたられる
antic おふざけ

Nazi". (This refers to an episode in which the characters meet a rude owner of a soup restaurant.)

I am not an expert in pasta. I caused great amusement once when I asked a waiter what fusilli is. "Don't you remember fusilli Jerry?" my friend asked. (Apparently, Kramer once made a tiny sculpture of Jerry using fusilli.)

Occasionally, *Seinfeld* has come up with something useful. I like the word "regifting", for when someone passes a present they received on to someone else. (I think this happens quite often in Japan.) But I dislike other expressions and catchphrases that were made popular by *Seinfeld*. "Yada, yada, yada..." irritates me. (It just means "and so on" or "etcetera".)

Seinfeld claimed to be "a show about nothing", meaning it didn't try to address big issues but rather portrayed the eccentric interactions that can occur between friends and the banalities of everyday life: being hungry and not being able to get into a restaurant, wanting to leave a party but having to stay a while to be polite, having to break up with someone...

It seems that one of the little topics covered was "double dipping". This, I learned, is when people share a plate of, say, hummus and someone dips with their pita bread, takes a bite and then dips again. Thanks to *Seinfeld*, everyone in New York knows to confirm in advance with your fellow diners whether it's okay to "double dip". (This particular piece of etiquette was unknown to me.)

The problem for me is that *Seinfeld* ran for nine series and 190 episodes. That's a lot to catch up on, especially since I find the show rather dated and not consistently funny.

Vocabulary

fusilli フジッリ［らせん状にねじれた形のパスタ］
banality 陳腐、凡庸
hummus ホムス［ピタパンに塗って食べる中近東のペースト］
pita bread ピタパン［中近東の丸く平たいパン］

An Englishman in N.Y.

I don't want to watch them all, so it seems I am doomed to be excluded by my inability to spot *Seinfeld* references.

My worst *Seinfeld*-related problem came when I suggested to an American ex-girlfriend that I wanted to remain "pals". I don't know why I used that word; normally I would have just said "friends". But it seemed to particularly annoy her. A month later I happened to learn that when Jerry was trying to create distance between himself and his ex-girlfriend Elaine she was infuriated by his suggestion that they were "pals".

Somehow, the fact this had been on *Seinfeld* made what I had done worse. People in New York expect that everyone knows that you don't double dip—and you never call your ex-girlfriend a "pal".

Vocabulary
doomed to... …することを悪く運命づけられて
inability 無力、無能

World Cup Woes

June 12th, 2010 is not a day I wish to remember. But it is a day that I will, unfortunately, not be able to forget easily. As football fans may know, on that day England were held to a 1-1 draw by the US in the South Africa World Cup. England then went on to finish 2nd in their group behind the US, which meant we had to play a confident young German team in the next round—and lost 4-1. This woeful performance and early exit plunged the nation into a state of near-mourning over the death of English football.

Vocabulary
woe 悲哀
plunge （ある状態に）陥れる
state of near-mourning 服喪中に近い状態

It was terrible to lose 4-1 to the Germans. But for me personally, it was a disaster to manage only a draw with the US. I had spent a long time telling American friends that their team was "not bad" and "improving", but that they would be no match for England. Naturally, on June 13th I got a few mocking emails and phone calls from those same friends.

The truth is I actually feared all along England could lose. The English have always believed themselves far better at football than they actually are. There are two main reasons for this. One is that we invented the game of football in its modern version in the 19th century. The second reason is that once, in 1966, England actually won the World Cup.

Any rational person can easily see that neither of those things have much relevance to the present state of English football. But we English somehow think we have a right to do well at major tournaments. (It is almost heresy to mention this, but the one time England won the World Cup in 1966 there were only 16 teams at the Finals and England had the important advantage of playing every game at their home stadium of Wembley in London.)

So I have always had doubts about whether England is really a great footballing nation or merely a team with a strong football tradition. But I desperately wanted at least for England to beat the US because it is still one thing we *should* be better at than them.

Our beloved game, which we gave to the world, isn't anywhere near being the favourite sport in America. It comes behind American

Vocabulary
no match for... …にかなわない・及びもつかない
mocking ちゃかした
rational 理性的な
relevance 関連性
heresy 異論

football, baseball and basketball of course, but even ice hockey has a similar level of popularity. They don't even call it by its real name, instead referring to "soccer". I once saw an advertisement for a sports bar in New Jersey that listed the sports it showed. NASCAR was named ahead of "soccer" (with skiing and swimming next on the list). In 2010, the Americans did better at their fourth favourite sport than we did at our number one sport.

There are committed football fans in the US, but many Americans see it as a sport played mainly by girls, immigrants and college students. Since the US team did well, many Americans—with their special brand of patriotism—proudly adopted the team as shining example of their nation's greatness. If they had done badly, I suspect most Americans would have just shrugged it off.

It's different for the English. We care deeply about doing so badly. The worst thing is that this was considered a chance for England to avenge its most humiliating defeat ever. The only other time England have played the US in a competitive game of football was in the 1950 World Cup, when a makeshift team of American college kids beat a professional team of English 1-0. Now, sixty years on, we have done worse than the Americans at another World Cup. As a sports fan, I have to applaud the achievement of the US team. But as an England fan I don't have to like it.

Vocabulary
patriotism 愛国心
shrug ... off （侮辱など）を無視し去る・振り捨てる
avenge かたきをとる
makeshift team 急造のチーム

My Personal Ten Best Things About Living in New York

Free concerts

I have seen Verdi operas performed in Central Park, listened to a string quartet play Schoenberg in the courtyard of the Museum of Modern Art, watched films while picnicking on the grass below the Brooklyn Bridge... and never paid a penny for the privilege. New York is particularly blessed with free events; it's not just quantity but quality.

Brunch

You can eat brunch in any American (and many non-American) cities. But in New York Sunday brunch is very much an institution. For me, it's an economical way to sample a restaurant I might not normally be able to afford. A recent memorable brunch for me was in a restaurant near Wall Street, gorgeously converted from an old bank vault, where I washed down a gourmet burger with Guinness and Bloody Mary for $20 including tip—enough fuel to last me for the rest of the day.

Rivers and bridges

Manhattan is an island, of course, but Brooklyn and Queens are also located on an island (Long Island). Then there is Staten Island and Governor's Island. It stands to reason that there is a lot of waterfront in New York and plenty of bridges. There are hundreds of spots from which to view the water and the city. The magnificent bridges serve both as part of the view and ideal vantage points.

Vocabulary

courtyard 中庭
privilege 恩恵
vault （銀行の）金庫室
enough fuel to last 十分に持続するだけの燃料
vantage point 眺望のきく地点

The Floating Pool Lady

I didn't quite understand my friend when he told me there was a swimming pool in the East River near his house. But he was right. It's a pool built into a floating barge and every summer it is towed to a spot in the river so that people can swim hygienically (and for free). For one glorious summer it was near me in Brooklyn, but since then has been located in the Bronx.

Gyms

You don't have to walk more than a few blocks to find a gym in New York. If you are disciplined enough to go more than once a week, they are reasonably priced and help you keep exercising during the freezing months of winter and the humid summer months.

The Waterfront Greenway cycle path

You can ride almost uninterrupted for 32

miles around the edge of Manhattan. (Only at a few points are you required to share the road with traffic.) Personally, I would sometimes ride across the Williamsburg Bridge to Manhattan, join the Greenway on the Lower East Side, round the southern tip of Manhattan and back up the Hudson River on the west side to around 14th Street, where I would fold my bicycle back up and get on the subway home. A glorious way to spend a couple of hours.

The 30-day MTA pass

New York public transport isn't perfect, but it is a bargain. And for $89 the 30-day pass gives you unlimited travel across the city. For anyone with the time and inclination to explore the city, that works out as pennies per ride.

Vocabulary
barge 平底の荷船
be towed （舟が）曳かれて進む
hygienically 衛生的に、清潔に

Strand book store

This sprawling store near Union Square is a browser's paradise. New Yorkers tend to read intelligent books and then tend to sell them on, rather than have them clogging up their small apartments. Many of those books find their way to the Strand—and many of them are put on sale for just $1.

Fairway Market

For a big city, New York isn't blessed with great supermarkets. The upmarket ones are very pricey, and the cheap ones have a poor selection (and aren't that cheap). Fairway is the exception: it has a great range of quality foodstuffs at fair prices, including lots of fresh fruit and vegetables. My favourite branch is in Red Hook, with an outside seating area looking across the harbour to the Statue of Liberty. What better way to have lunch than to buy some fresh bread and cheese and consume it right there?

Century 21

There are lots of department stores in the city. Century 21 is a big, crazy, crowded one that always has thousands of bargains. When it has a sale on, prices are further reduced still; and my wardrobe heaves with shirts I snapped up here.

Vocabulary

sprawling だだっ広い
browser 立ち読みする人、店内をぶらぶら見て回る人
sell on 転売する
clog up （場所を）ふさぐ
upmarket 高級な
heave 膨れる
snap up 先を争って買う

My Personal Ten Worst Things About Living in New York

Drying clothes

Probably fewer than one apartment in a hundred in New York has a space where you can hang out your clothes to dry naturally. So instead you have to pay to put them through the tumble dryer, which can damage delicate materials, is environmentally wasteful and gives you a jumbled mess of hot, electrically charged clothes at the end. And even then some clothing, like thick socks and jeans, still come out slightly damp.

Tipping for drinks

I have never quite grasped why I should pay an extra dollar for someone to turn on a tap, turn it off again and place a drink on the counter. It's pretty much compulsory to pay the tip, so it is not really a reward for good service. And

I dislike the way you always get your change in $1 bills to make sure you have a supply to tip with.

"Third World" traffic

Lots of big cities have a traffic problem but New York seems to have an unusual number of horn-sounding, crazy drivers. I think it's because the city has a constant supply of newcomers, many of whom work as taxi drivers, from countries where reckless, noisy driving is the norm. And then New York makes them a bit crankier.

Vocabulary
jumbled mess ぐちゃぐちゃに散らかった状態
grasp 理解する
compulsory 強制的な
reckless 無謀な
cranky 怒りっぽい

The G train

Some of the subway lines in New York are quite reliable. Others are a bit sporadic. But the worst, by some distance, is the G train. It's supposed to run every ten minutes or so, but you can easily end up waiting 25 minutes.

Worse still, the train runs a "crosstown" route between Brooklyn and Queens that no other train does. So although you can never be sure when the G train will come, it's still marginally better than the alternative of getting a train into Manhattan and then back out again. Little wonder people say "Oh Gee!" when talking about the G train.

Cutting nails on the subway

A lot of people complain that there is litter on the subway, or that it is noisy with too many people. All of those things are true, but what really drives me mad is when people cut their nails on the train. It doesn't happen often but it does happen. When I hear that distinctive "clip clip" sound my shoulders instinctively tense in irritation.

Psychobabble

New Yorkers use a lot of jargon from psychoanalysis. People are variously described as "in denial", "anal", "OCD", "self-medicating", "seeking closure", "acting out" and "passive aggressive". Very occasionally this is helpful, but these expressions grate because they are overused and often used inaccurately.

Vocabulary
sporadic 不規則でばらばらの
psychobabble 心理学用語を使ったわけのわからない話し方
jargon （仲間内で用いる）特殊用語
anal 肛門期の
OCD 強迫性障害
act out （抑圧されていた感情を）無意識に行動化する
grate かんに障る

Sex and the City

It's upsetting to find that tens of thousands of people all around you love something that you hate. I find *SATC* to be false and populated with shallow, boring, self-obsessed people whose standards of behaviour I deplore. It makes me feel very isolated when I hear that people "associate with" this or that character in the show, or that they look up to the characters and aspire to their lifestyles.

Supermarkets that don't sell wine

Because of antiquated licensing laws you can't buy wine in supermarkets. Which means that once you have got all your food shopping, you sometimes have to struggle a few more blocks with your bags to a wine store and queue up again. And beware: sometimes supermarkets sell a strange, weird-tasting low alcohol wine that must have been invented especially for supermarkets.

Catlessness

Okay, "catlessness" isn't a real word but if it did exist it would nearly describe the situation in New York. I love cats but very rarely see one in New York, except the occasional semi-stray which is being fed by local people. No wonder there are so many rodents in New York.

The Post Office

My friend once described American post offices as "the last refuge of Communist bureaucracy". The branches are almost always in ugly grey buildings. You always have to queue up and there are endless rules about what you

Vocabulary
self-obsessed 自己執着の
deplore 遺憾に思う
antiquated 古くから続いている
rodent げっし動物 [ネズミやリスなど]
Communist bureaucracy 共産主義のお役所仕事

can and can't do. There are very precise rules, for example, about exactly where you write the address and return address. I once walked in with a package and was given three reasons why I couldn't post it: "wrong kind of tape", "wrong shape of package" and "you can't reuse an Amazon box".

The Joys of Storage

One day when I was riding the train through Brooklyn I saw a huge sign saying "Treasure Island". I was intrigued partly because I find it amusing when companies give themselves grandiloquent names. But also because I had just been thinking about the growing amount of clutter in my house.

Treasure Island is one of several "self storage" facilities that cater to people in New York. A lot of its custom is from small businesses that need a secure place to store inventory. But a growing number of customers are people like

Vocabulary
be intrigued 興味を抱く
grandiloquent 大げさな
clutter がらくた
cater 提供する
inventory 在庫品

me, who can't seem to reconcile their acquisitive nature with their limited living space.

I have stored my stuff once before when I lived in Japan, in a god-forsaken place miles from the nearest station—and a very, very long way from my apartment in Tokyo. In New York, it was entirely different. It was urban storage. Obviously, the location wasn't prime real estate but I could get there on the subway in half an hour, which meant it was possible to visit regularly, not just for storing and redeeming on a one-off basis.

Obviously, the main advantage of storage is that New York apartments are small so it's good to have somewhere to put your stuff. I paid $30 a month for a tiny storage space. An extra room in my apartment would have cost, I estimate, $400 a month.

"Decluttering" is something of a buzzword these days. There are TV shows and websites with tips on how to get rid of stuff. I understand the attraction of having a sparse, clear look to your apartment. But I also like having lots of stuff and hate throwing away anything useful. Self storage squares the circle for me.

At the very least, I do two big transfers of stuff a year. The seasons in New York are quite extreme—boiling in summer, freezing in winter—so there comes a moment when all my T-shirts get neatly packed away and out come my coats and sweaters. A lot of people, I notice, use their storage space for ski equipment. Apparently, this is one of the things that people like to own but hate to have in the house.

I am a bargain hunter so I tend to buy

Vocabulary

acquisitive nature 欲張りな性質
god-forsaken place 人里離れた場所
redeem 取り戻す
one-off 1回限りの
buzzword 流行語、宣伝文句
sparse (物が) 少ない
square the circle 一見、不可能なことを企てる

clothes at a big discount as they go out of season. Friends say to me that it doesn't make sense to buy something that you won't use for another six months. But it has never struck me as a problem because I have somewhere out of the way to put it until that time.

There is one major reason storage has been useful for me personally. I have never settled in one apartment all the time I have been in New York, but have moved from place to place every four to six months. If I chose to move to a small apartment, I can simply put a bit more in storage. Or if I find a large place that is a bargain, I can bring out more of my possessions. Once, I was even able to cram all my stuff in storage for a few weeks between apartments while I went on holiday. The rent I saved was more than the cost of the trip.

It may sound a bit strange but I really enjoyed visiting my storage facility. I have always liked old industrial buildings, and this was the first one that I had a sort of stake in. I thought of it as *my warehouse*. And I liked going there because it meant I was having a mini-makeover in my life. I would be bringing books that I had read to change for books that I wanted to read. I would be swapping over some of my art works (mostly woodblock prints that I bought in Japan), so that my walls at home would look a bit different. And I would be changing the clothes I wear (usually bringing out a few items that I had bought in last year's sales and never worn).

Sometimes I would even be surprised to discover something nice that I had bought and forgotten about. Or I would be struck anew by a piece of art that I hadn't looked at in a while. At moments like that I would think the name Treasure Island was quite apt.

Vocabulary
have a stake in 利害関係がある、関心がある
mini-makeover ちょっとした模様替え・改装

Mind the Gap

People sometimes assume that living in a foreign country is hard because of the "culture clash" that you may experience. It can be difficult to find that your values are fundamentally different from those of the people around you. But it can also be amusing to find small, sometimes comical differences in the way people think, act and speak. We tend to think of common sense as universal, but quite often it's something that is specific to one country.

I was staying with my friend in New Jersey when his son came down from bed saying he couldn't sleep because he was hungry. His dad then told him he could have some cheese from the fridge, but nothing else. I was amazed because in England it is "common sense" that you must not eat cheese before bedtime. It is, in fact, the only thing that everyone in England will tell you *not* to eat late at night "because it gives you nightmares". In America, I learned, cheese is seen as "easily digestible" and therefore the ideal thing to have before bedtime.

I was being given a tour of a museum once and as part of the lecture the tour guide asked people what they do when they feel unwell. Several of the Americans mentioned "drink ginger ale". This turns out to be standard wisdom in the US, but in England you would be considered daft if you thought that fizzy pop was a good idea for someone who is ill.

Once in America I was prescribed antibiotics. I was annoyed that the doctor didn't warn me not to drink alcohol until the treatment was

Vocabulary
culture clash 文化の衝突
daft ばかな
fizzy pop 炭酸飲料
be prescribed antibiotics 抗生物質を処方される

over. In England it is universally believed that you must completely avoid alcohol when on antibiotics. But when the doctor didn't mention it I looked it up and it turns out that there is no particular interaction between alcohol and antibiotics. So drinking in moderation is fine. The English believe you are risking your life to mix them, and now I can't resist teasing English friends by telling them that I need a beer because I want to get rid of the nasty taste of the antibiotics.

Attitudes to office parties vary greatly depending on the country. In England (and Japan) it's quite normal for people to cut loose a bit, i.e. have a few drinks and speak your mind. In America, this would be fraught with danger. You would get a bad workplace reputation if you drank more than two drinks and you should never, ever say what you think about your boss. This amuses me because it is supposed to be America that is the "free" and "democratic" culture, and the English and Japanese who are a bit "repressed".

I am regularly intrigued by little differences in language. I knew that Americans say "in back of" instead of "behind", but only recently did I hear that some Americans prefer to use this because they think "behind" is a bit rude (it's another word for "bum", but actually a euphemism).

An English friend and I mail each other whenever we come across amusing pronunciations. He started it when he spotted how Americans say "yurrup" to mean Europe, and the word "warrior" is pronounced "woyyer", to rhyme with "lawyer".

Vocabulary
cut loose はめを外す
fraught with danger 危険に満ちた
repressed 抑圧された
bum 尻

The first time I heard an American pronounce the name "Graham" I made her repeat it because she said "Gramm", rather than "Gray-am" as we English do. There is a popular brand of crackers called Graham, and I lived near to Graham Avenue station for a while, so I heard this word a surprising amount.

My favourite odd pronunciation is the word "buoy". We pronounce it the same as "boy" but for Americans it is "boo-ee". I try to create situations in which they have to say this word for me, when I am near the waterfront for example. "Is that a man swimming out there?" I ask. "No, I think it's just a boo-ee," they say.

Americans are themselves amused by these little differences. A friend told me how his colleagues at the Chicago office would say, "Hey we haven't seen you for over a fortnight," and then laugh. It confused him because they would say it whether it had been a month or six months since his last visit. One day he realised that Americans don't have the word "fortnight" (it means two weeks) and had been tickled by it.

Vocabulary
be tickled おもしろがる

PROFILE

Colin Joyce was born in Essex, England in 1970. He studied Ancient and Modern History at Oxford University before winning a scholarship to study in Kobe. He always wanted to learn a second language, but didn't realise it would take him almost a decade in Japan before his Japanese became "quite good". In Tokyo he wrote for *Newsweek Japan* magazine and was correspondent for the English newspaper *The Daily Telegraph*.

He moved to New York in 2007 in a belated attempt to achieve his dream of living in several different countries while still a young man. He stayed for over three years, working as a freelance writer, during which he wrote the essays in this book.

He is the author of several books. 『「ニッポン社会」入門』, 『「アメリカ社会」入門』, 『「イギリス社会」

入門』, all published by NHK Publishing, Inc., contain observations from his experience of life in those three countries. The first and last of these are also available in English, titled *How to Japan* and *Let's England*.

He is a lover of beer and football and has a huge collection of books that he intends to read one day, when the world runs out of beer and football. He currently lives in Essex, the place he always wanted to leave as a boy.

An Englishman in N.Y.
Bites on the Big Apple

2011（平成 23）年 11 月 10 日　第 1 刷発行
2015（平成 27）年 2 月 25 日　第 2 刷発行

著者	コリン・ジョイス
	©2011 Colin Joyce
発行者	溝口明秀
発行所	NHK 出版
	〒150-8081　東京都渋谷区宇田川町 41-1
	電話　0570-002-046（編集）
	0570-000-321（注文）
	ホームページ　　http://www.nhk-book.co.jp
	振替　00110-1-49701
印刷	文唱堂／近代美術
製本	田中製本

落丁・乱丁本はお取り替えいたします。
定価はカバーに表示してあります。

本書の無断複写（コピー）は、著作権法上の例外を除き、
著作権侵害となります。

Printed in Japan
ISBN 978-4-14-035097-3 C0082

装丁・本文デザイン	畑中 猛
DTP	ドルフィン
校正	筧 万理子

本書は NHK「ラジオ英会話」2008 年 4 月号〜 2011 年 3 月号のテキストに連載されたエッセイの中から抜粋し、加筆・訂正したものです。